Teen
uncover the
REAL YOU

Teen
uncover the
REAL YOU

HEARST BOOKS
A division of Sterling Publishing Co., Inc.

New York / London
www.sterlingpublishing.com

Library of Congress Cataloging-in-Publication Data
Teen uncover the real you : a quiz book / the editors of Teen magazine.
    p. cm.
 Includes bibliographical references and index.
 ISBN 978-1-58816-743-9 (alk. paper)
 1. Teenage girls–Psychology–Miscellanea. 2. Preteens–Psychology–
Miscellanea. 3. Girls–Psychology–Miscellanea. [1. Questions and
answers.] I. Teen (New York, N.Y.)
 HQ798.T397 2008
 155.5'33–dc22

                         2008011839

10 9 8 7 6 5 4 3 2 1

Book design by Margaret Rubiano

Published by Hearst Books
A Division of Sterling Publishing Co., Inc.
387 Park Avenue South, New York, NY 10016

Teen and *Hearst Books* are trademarks of Hearst Communications, Inc.

www.teenmag.com

For information about custom editions, special sales, premium and
corporate purchases, please contact Sterling Special Sales Department
at 800-805-5489 or specialsales@sterlingpublishing.com.

Distributed in Canada by Sterling Publishing
C/o Canadian Manda Group, 165 Dufferin Street
Toronto, Ontario, Canada M6K 3H6

Distributed in Australia by Capricorn Link (Australia) Pty. Ltd.
P. O. Box 704, Windsor, NSW 2756 Australia

Manufactured in China

Sterling ISBN 978-1-58816-743-9

foreword

Welcome to the first-ever *Teen* quiz book, "Uncover the Real You." *Teen* magazine has always been into helping you discover your true self—that amazing, insanely cool girl who is YOU. Yes, you!

So, how do *Teen* quizzes help? They help you figure out who you are; they reveal your strengths and your weaknesses, your quirks and your powers. Sometimes they even uncover clues about your relationships, like how well you know your friends, or whether a guy is right for you. Quizzes decipher bits of information that help you understand yourself and how to deal with your life.

Some quizzes you'll want to take by yourself, others are best when taken with a friend. It's up to you to decide. The important thing is to have a good time, be open-minded, and remember, it's not about the right answer—it's about YOUR answer. That's how you uncover the real you! So get ready to discover things about yourself you never knew before. Enjoy the adventure and be prepared for surprises.

Love,
a. The *Teen* crew
b. Some fellow quiz lovers
c. Your favorite magazine staff
d. All of the above.

P.S. The answer is d.

are you a go-getter?

Do you make the most of every chance you're given or do you let opportunity pass you by?

1 The guy you like is at the track meet. There's an open space next to him on the bleachers and you need a place to sit. You:
a. Walk over to suss out how awkward it would be to sit there.
b. Sit nearby with friends—c'mon, you'd look stupid being all by yourself.
c. Quickly get over there and snag the spot by him.

2 You get a mass e-mail from a friend of a friend who's starting a band and looking for people to audition. You play the drums so you:
a. Save the e-mail. Maybe you'll ask your friend about it later.
b. Delete the e-mail. You don't even know this girl.
c. E-mail the chick back to find out what kind of music the group plays.

3 There's a hot new guy in school and your English teacher asks who'd like to help him get caught up on the book you've been reading. Do you volunteer?
a. Yes, before some other girl gets to him.
b. Probably not. It isn't your style.
c. You raise your hand, but half hope you won't be chosen.

4 A friend leaves her iPod at your house. You:
a. Put it in your bag to give back to her the next day.
b. Scroll through and check out her music before returning it.
c. Ask if you can swap iPods for a while, so you can listen to some new stuff.

5. Your parents decide to take scuba diving lessons and offer to pay for you to learn, too. Do you do it?

a. Of course! Scuba seems so cool.

b. Nope—that means you'd have to hang with the 'rents.

c. Yes, but only after they harass you about it.

6. There's an extra-credit mini essay question at the end of a super-long history exam. How much effort do you give it?

a. A lot—it could make a big difference to your grade.

b. Some—you'll give it a shot because it's not like a wrong answer will count against you.

c. Hardly any—who has any energy after that difficult test?

7. You're at a street fair with your buds and you see a booth selling garlic ice cream. Do you try some?

a. Only if everyone else does.

b. It's unlikely.

c. Totally!

8. Your friend's parents are big into going to the symphony. They have extra tickets for a performance and your bud asks if you would like to go, even though it's not really your thing. Do you?

a. No way! It's probably super boring.

b. Sure, if you don't have anything better to do.

c. Definitely. There must be a reason why people love it.

scoring

1. a. 2; b. 1; c. 3 2. a. 3; b. 1; c. 3 3. a. 3; b. 1; c. 2 4. a. 1; b. 2; c. 3 5. a. 3; b. 1; c. 2 6. a. 3; b. 2; c. 1 7. a. 2; b. 1; c. 3 8. a. 1; b. 2; c. 3

scoring

go-getter girl

20 to 24 points

For you, life is like a buffet and you're first in line, trying every dish. We totally love that attitude. There are so many great chances in life, as long as one recognizes them—and you do! You're motivated and curious about everything, whether it's new music, new people, or new food. You grab almost every opportunity that comes your way—just don't overextend yourself. Sure, sampling all the buffet has to offer is great, but it's just as crucial to know when to stop before it becomes too much!

mildly motivated

13 to 19 points

You take a chance once in a while, but you're not exactly a go-getter. Why not? Maybe fear or embarrassment is holding you back. Don't let it! Someone once said that when people look back on their lives, they usually regret the things they didn't do, not the things they did. How lame would you feel if you didn't get the guy you liked because another girl got his attention first? Or you weren't a part of a rockin' band because you didn't bother to audition? Next time you have an opportunity, grab it!

miss'd opportunities

8 to 12 points

Sadly, life might be passing you by. Think of all the fun people you could be meeting and all the awesome experiences you'd be having if you said "yes" more often. We're not suggesting you agree to every crazy idea out there, but be more open to trying something different. Even little things like extra-credit questions are opportunities (to raise your grade or just impress your teacher). And most importantly, if you don't go after what you want, your chances of getting it are way slimmer!

do you like you?

You know what you think of your lab partner (uh, she's kinda snooty) or your best friend (love her, of course!) but how do you feel about you? Take this quiz to find out if you're your own biggest fan or worst enemy.

1 You're finally getting chatty with that hot guy from third period when he says your favorite band is "completely lame." You:

a. Keep quiet. If this gorgeous guy thinks the band sucks, then maybe it does.

b. Tell him he has no taste in tunes and list reasons why the band rocks.

c. Smile, but tell him you own—and love—all their CDs.

2 Your dream is to live in Paris. You even joined the French Club at school. One day, you hear one of the popular girls talking about the "French Freaks." You:

a. Decide she's an uncultured American idiot.

b. Realize she might be right.

c. Laugh it off—who cares what she thinks?

3 You're at the carnival with your two best buds. You all decide to go on a ride, but it's your turn to sit alone. Wait! There's an adorable hottie in line! What's your move?

a. Smile and say, "I've got an open seat."

b. Insist he sit with you and don't take no for an answer!

c. You hope he doesn't look in your direction.

4 Using these blank spaces, write down three things you like about yourself.

_I'__ ___ ___ _____ _ ___ __ ___
_____ _ ___ ____ _ ___ __
_MY_ __ __ _____ words_

Don't read the rest of this question until you're finished. Now, how hard was that?

a. Pretty hard. I could barely think of three things!

b. Simple. I could've listed at least five.

c. No problem once I got into it.

5 Which of the following statements best describes what you just wrote about yourself?

a. I wrote about my looks and/or my possessions.

b. I wrote about my talents and/or personality.

c. I wrote a mix of stuff.

6 You're out to eat with your family when you lock eyes with a cute boy in the next booth. Your dad starts one of his terrible jokes. You:

a. Wish your parents would stop messing up your life.

b. Blush and tell your dad to stop being weird in public.

c. Let Dad finish his joke and give him a little laugh at the end.

7 If you could take a pill that would make you skinnier, smarter and prettier, BUT you'd lose half of your memories (and you can't pick which ones), would you do it?

a. Yes.

b. No.

8 Your mom asks if you want to go shopping with her. You agree, but only if:

a. She agrees to go to your favorite lunch spot.

b. You go somewhere you won't run into people you know.

c. She won't make you try stuff on in front of those horrible department store mirrors.

9 You give yourself credit for your accomplishments and forgive your faults pretty quickly.

a. True.

b. False.

10 A friend from another school invites you to a party. You won't know anyone there besides her, so you decide to:

a. Stay home and watch reruns. No one will wanna talk to you if they don't know you.

b. Go for it. Maybe you'll meet some cool people and have a good time.

c. Skip it. They could be total dorks for all you know.

11 The *Victoria's Secret* catalog makes you think:

a. I'm so fat. I might as well eat a pint of chocolate ice cream!

b. Starting tomorrow, I'm gonna work out, stop having dessert, and give myself a makeover!

c. I may never be a supermodel, but I'm talented, interesting, and have great (fill-in-the-blank)

_____.

scoring

1. a. 1; b. 3; c. 2 2. a. 3; b. 1; c. 2 3. a. 2; b. 3; c. 1 4. a. 1; b. 3; c. 2 5. a. 1; b. 3; c. 2 6. a. 3; b. 1; c. 2 7. a. 3; b. 1 8. a. 2; b. 3; c. 1 9. a. 3; b. 1 10. a. 1; b. 2; c. 3 11. a. 1; b. 3; c. 2

scoring

too-proud princess

25 to 33 points

You're confident and strong, but underneath the brassy exterior, you may have a lot of self-doubt. To avoid looking or feeling embarrassed, you sometimes put down anyone who might make you feel less than confident. You don't want to seem weak, so you build walls. Be careful, though, because the impression you're giving people is that you're too proud and too pushy. It's time to let your defenses down. Start by focusing on your best qualities, like your sense of humor or artistic talent. Whatever it is, give yourself some credit. Once you do, you might find you've started to like yourself for real.

satisfied sister

18 to 24 points

You know who you are and you're happy with yourself, for the most part. You seem to get it that the more you like yourself, the more appealing you are to others. When you feel good about who you are, you give off a confident vibe and people are drawn to you, which makes you feel even better! Of course, you realize you have faults, but who doesn't? You can get down about things, like a bad test score or a guy not liking you or a zit on your nose, but you manage to put those things in perspective. So give yourself a pat on the back. Nice work!

critical cutie

11 to 17 points

It's one thing to be modest, but you really don't like yourself sometimes. It's totally normal to feel awkward or unattractive at this stage in your life. After all, no one said being a teen was easy. But give yourself a break! There's no need to be overly self-critical. You're probably way cuter and more awesome than you give yourself credit for!

scoring

too-proud princess

25 to 33 points

You're confident and strong, but underneath the brassy exterior, you may have a lot of self-doubt. To avoid looking or feeling embarrassed, you sometimes put down anyone who might make you feel less than confident. You don't want to seem weak, so you build walls. Be careful, though, because the impression you're giving people is that you're too proud and too pushy. It's time to let your defenses down. Start by focusing on your best qualities, like your sense of humor or artistic talent. Whatever it is, give yourself some credit. Once you do, you might find you've started to like yourself for real.

satisfied sister

18 to 24 points

You know who you are and you're happy with yourself, for the most part. You seem to get it that the more you like yourself, the more appealing you are to others. When you feel good about who you are, you give off a confident vibe and people are drawn to you, which makes you feel even better! Of course, you realize you have faults, but who doesn't? You can get down about things, like a bad test score or a guy not liking you or a zit on your nose, but you manage to put those things in perspective. So give yourself a pat on the back. Nice work!

critical cutie

11 to 17 points

It's one thing to be modest, but you really don't like yourself sometimes. It's totally normal to feel awkward or unattractive at this stage in your life. After all, no one said being a teen was easy. But give yourself a break! There's no need to be overly self-critical. You're probably way cuter and more awesome than you give yourself credit for!

psst! can you keep a secret?

When it comes to juicy gossip and ultrasensitive info, can you keep your lips locked? This quiz reveals your secret-keeping status!

1 Your best friend spills the beans about her latest crush. The trouble is, he was flirting with you a few minutes ago. You:
a. Play wide-eyed and innocent. Who knows, maybe he was just being friendly.
b. Ask about the cutie in her math class. Hey, nothing wrong with diverting her attention, right?
c. Dish the dirt—ASAP! Hello, your friend can do a million times better.

2 Sources say the hottest guy in school is about to dump his girlfriend. You:
a. Keep it on the DL because it's none of your business.
b. Mention it to your good pal, but warn her that you have no idea whether it's true.
c. Automatically send a red alert e-mail to everyone you know. This is HUGE and you can't keep it under wraps!

3 A good friend suddenly confesses she might be failing chemistry. You:
a. Promise to keep her secret safe. Then wonder what she's gonna do.
b. Report the facts to your older brother because he's a chem whiz and he might be able to help.
c. Accidentally blurt the news to your boyfriend and all of his friends. (Dang! You forgot it was a secret.)

4 You totally hit it off with a major hottie at the pizza party last night. Your friends are desperately drilling you for details. You:
a. Refuse to comment—you like to keep that stuff to yourself.
b. Give a little shrug, hinting that there might be a spark.
c. Wait until you have everyone's undivided attention, then slowly rehash your convo, minute-by-minute.

5 RUMOR ALERT: The geeky guy in algebra has a crush on the teacher. You:

a. Roll your eyes. Who cares?
b. Giggle about it behind closed doors with your best pals.
c. Nod your head knowingly 'cause you started it.

6 It's your little sister's birthday next week and your mom is surprising her with a puppy. You:

a. Say nothing. She's going to be so surprised!
b. Drop a couple hints just to drive her crazy. (She'll never ever guess!)
c. Immediately grab her arm and shriek, "Oh my God! You're getting a puppy!"

7 To you, "Don't tell a soul" means:

a. MY LIPS ARE SEALED!
b. I won't say a peep unless I absolutely, positively have to.
c. Fresh gossip. Where's my cell? Can't wait to give all the girls the scoop.

8 Let's face it, glossy gossip mags are:

a. Ugh, total trash.
b. Fun to flip through when you're zoning out.
c. A complete and utter obsession. In fact, you can barely pry your fingers away to finish your homework.

9 Admit it. You're famous for being:

a. A fab listener. Friends can tell you anything.
b. Cool to hang with. You hardly ever talk trash.
c. The go-to girl for all things secretive.

10 No doubt about it, secrets are:

a. 100% sacred.
b. Important.
c. Sooo much fun to spill.

Before you spill someone else's secret, close your mouth and count to 10. As you do the numbers, think how you would feel if your bud spilled your secret.

scoring

queen of quiet

Wow! Hear no evil, speak no evil, that's you. You're a girl who knows how to keep her lips zipped. Warning: Be careful about staying too quiet. While being a secret-keeper is a great trait, sometimes it's best to speak up, like if you know something that could hurt or help a friend. Your pal will respect you even more for watching her back.

discreet diva

Congratulations. When it comes to secrets, you know when to talk and when to balk. You've mastered the art of how to treat people and their privacy—with respect. You understand that some things you're privy to can never, ever be divulged. Other times? Well, let's just say that you know how to use discretion (wink, wink).

blabber babe

Easy there, girlfriend! Your mouth is running on overdrive. Sure, it's fun to always be "in the know," but that doesn't give you the right to blab everyone else's business 24/7. FYI: You might be starting to get a rep. Maybe it's time to give it a rest. After all, you do want to keep your friends, right?

are your buds holding you back?

Are you a follower or happy to stand on your own? Take our quiz to find out if being one of the crowd is your thing.

1 Right this second, your blog contains messages from:
a. Only your closest and tightest friends.
b. Ten or so people from different groups.
c. Enough individuals who don't know each other to cast a seriously kooky reality show.

2 A real friend is:
a. Fiercely loyal, no matter what.
b. Fun to hang with.
c. Someone who helps you to be the best you can be.

3 If your pals were bashing a girl you thought was sweet but not part of your gang, you'd:
a. Keep quiet.
b. Crack a joke about how the last time you checked, nobody was perfect.
c. Stick up for her.

4 Everyone you know is waking up super early to get in line for tickets to the *American Idol* concert, but you're eyeing the Warped Tour. With only enough cash for one ticket, you:
a. Choose *Idol*.
b. Wait with your buds for fun, but save your money.
c. Dig around school to find a group to go to Warped.

5 Would you have to check with your crowd before inviting someone new to crash with you at lunch?

a. Yeah, otherwise it would be weird.

b. A mention beforehand would be nice.

c. No—newbies are always welcome.

6 On *Gossip Girl,* you'd be:

a. Serena.

b. Blair.

c. Gossip who?

7 People need to dress a certain way in order to be part of your clique.

a. True.

b. Well, sometimes we follow the same trends, but usually we look totally different.

c. False.

8 OK, so your friends would say, "Grow up," but your guilty pleasure is *High School Musical.* You:

a. Secretly overheat your TiVo replaying it.

b. Try to sell your friends on the fact that Zac Efron is totally cute.

c. Blare the soundtrack and sing along with the car windows down as you exit the school parking lot.

tip

Ever watched *Mean Girls*? If not, rent the DVD and see what happens when you try too hard to fit in with the "in" crowd. The motto is: Be true to you!

scoring

groupie girl

You're part of a tight-knit circle of friends who probably dress and talk alike. While that may feel cozy for now, the truth is, your clique may be too close for comfort. It's likely your buds have so many inside jokes and private slang that it's hard for an outsider to understand, let alone get to know you. Kinda makes you think: Baskin-Robbins has 31 flavors and you're on a vanilla-only diet. Why? Time to broaden your friendship base. Reach out to an old pal or a cool classmate and see what happens.

not so clique-y

You've definitely got your girls, but they don't dictate your every move. Like, if you're in an iPod mood and they're feeling social, it's no biggie that you wanna zone out. However, your friends may not push you to take on new and different challenges that could have awesome rewards: Auditioning for a play or joining a sports team isn't their thing, but you might really love it. Take the time to find your groove and follow it. It makes your friendships—and your individuality—stronger.

friend to all

Your IM buddy list might seem weird to some because it's filled with friends from all kinds of classes, clubs and social circles. Some people find it tough to be without the security of an exclusive clique, but you're confident enough in your individuality to surround yourself with many types of buds whose company you enjoy. How cool is that? Very! Just be sure you aren't being a harsh judge of those who do choose to hang in crowds. Everybody's got her own taste.

are you loyal?

When it really matters, how tried-and-true are you?

1 You're getting dressed, putting on deodorant. What kind is it?
a. The same brand you've used for, like, ever.
b. Whatever the newest, best kind is.

2 You overhear someone saying your favorite band's last CD sucks. You:
a. Tell that fool he obviously doesn't have any taste.
b. Shrug, ignore him and keep walking.

3 You see a billboard for your favorite actor, but in a movie that looks super boring. Will you see the flick anyway?
a. Heck, yeah—the first week it's out!
b. Maybe, when it comes out on DVD.

4 After her boyfriend dumped her, you promised to go to the dance with your friend. But you get asked by a total cutie. You:
a. Tell the guy no because you promised to go with your bud.
b. Feel kinda bad, but accept the date.

5 Your friend's crush flirts with you. You:
a. Tell her about it immediately.
b. Flirt back, it's no biggie.

6 You and a pal copied the class brainiac's homework, but only your bud got caught. Do you fess up?
a. Yes, because your friend shouldn't suffer by herself.
b. No way! Why should both of you be punished?

7 You and your best friend have big plans, but her mom says she can't go until she cleans the house. Do you help?

a. Of course! The sooner it's clean, the sooner you're hitting the mall, movie theater, or whatever.

b. Why should you have to clean her house? Tell her you'll meet up later.

8 Your closest guy friend has a crush on an ultrapretty girl on your swim team. You:

a. Make sure to casually mention how amazing he is in front of her at practice.

b. Wish him luck and hope she likes him back.

9 You're at the mall with your sister after school and she gets into a shouting match with a girl in the food court. You:

a. Take your sister's side because family should always stick together.

b. Watch from the sidelines—you don't really know what it's about.

tip

There's a difference between being loyal and being a follower. Make sure your support is reciprocated!

scoring

miss loyal

You are the triedest and truest friend/girlfriend/sib around. You aren't just devoted to your loved ones, your loyalty extends to everything from bands to brands. You probably have the same sandwich for lunch nearly every day and have used the same shampoo for years. Being loyal to the people in your life is a fabulous quality, but trying new music, food, or even a new perfume keeps life exciting.

fairly faithful

Loyalty is all about being supportive, and most of the time you know how to be there when a bud needs you, but sometimes you can be a little fickle. Hey, nobody's perfect. The important thing is to be reliable when it really counts, and you're usually pretty good at figuring that out. Remember, your favorite bands won't be hurt if you don't stand by them when they're being dissed, but your sib or pal will!

disconnected diva

You're loyal to yourself and that's not a bad thing. You're simply faithful to your own wants and desires, which change quite often! It's cool that you like to try new things and avoid getting trapped in the same routine or stuck in a safe, cushy comfort zone. But you might want to be a little more dedicated to your friends and family. They need to know they can depend on you when things get tough.

do you obsess over your looks?

Caring about your appearance is one thing, but being a slave to your looks is another. Which kind of girl are you?

1 Admit it, getting ready for school in the morning is:

a. Easy breezy! Just pull your hair into a ponytail, wash your face, and go.

b. A little stressful, but fun. After all, you love getting creative, mixing and matching looks to show off your personality.

c. A total production, complete with special lighting, lotions, and music to go with your mood.

2 How often do you look in the mirror during the day?

a. Hmm, maybe once or twice? You don't really think about it.

b. Three or four times. You know, just to reapply your lip gloss.

c. Every chance you get! Mirrors, windows, shiny objects—you're constantly making sure your hair and makeup are in place.

3 During a softball game in PE, all you can think about is:

a. Woo-hoo! I hope we win.

b. I wish these uniforms were cuter, but whatever. I have more important things to worry about, like not dropping the ball.

c. Could these gym shorts be any more ugly? My crush will never notice me looking like this!

4 Yikes! It's picture day and you suddenly have a big, icky pimple. You:

a. Dab on some cover-up. It's not the end of the world.

b. Sulk to all your pals, but get the picture taken anyway. Maybe the photographer can retouch it.

c. Sob hysterically for an hour, then refuse to go to school no matter what your mom says.

5 You're primping for your BFF's party and you know your crush is going to be there. How many outfits do you try on?

a. Only one—it's just a party, not the red carpet.

b. Two, maybe three. After all, you want to look nice.

c. Um, hello! As many outfits as it takes to achieve your maximum gorgeousness, of course.

6 A professional mani/ pedi is:

a. Silly. Why pay big bucks when you can do it yourself at home?

b. A treat for special occasions.

c. A weekly must. Nothing makes you happier than thinking, "Wow, my nails look fab!"

7 You accidentally spill ketchup on your favorite white hoodie. You:

a. Laugh it off. It'll probably come out when you wash it.

b. Bolt to the bathroom. Maybe if you immediately scrub it with soap and water it won't stain.

c. Go into full crisis mode, whipping out your cell and pleading with your mom to bring you another top. You can't be seen like this!

8 Be honest: what's the one beauty item you simply can't live without?

a. Lip balm—dry lips are a bummer.

b. Probably mascara, to show off your eyes.

c. What? One? That's impossible to decide. Next question.

9 You're at the mall, and you and your pals pop into the beauty supply store. You immediately feel:

a. Overwhelmed and can't wait to leave.

b. Giddy—just look at the rows of eye shadows and lip liners.

c. Mesmerized. MUST. BUY. EVERYTHING.

scoring

beauty beginner

Talk about a low-maintenance girl! When it comes to your looks, you're about as natural as they come, and there's nothing wrong with that. It just shows you're confident with who you are. Make sure you're not missing out, though. You might want to consider brushing up on your beauty basics—a little mascara can make a huge difference. Who knows? You might even have fun.

groomin' girl

When it comes to your looks, you have a healthy relationship going. You definitely know how to work your way around a makeup counter, as well as twirl a curl with the best of 'em, but you don't go overboard. Appearances matter to you, but they're not everything. A bad hair day? That's not gonna get you down. Besides, in your book brains will always trump beauty.

appearance addicted

Step away from the mirror. We repeat: Step away from the mirror! Sure, looking fab is important, but your appearance is seriously starting to take over your life. Maybe you need to start focusing your energy elsewhere. Try reading a book, helping a friend with her homework, or even volunteering at a local pet shelter. Remember your inner beauty needs care, too.

the truth about guys

When you think of boys, what's the first thing that comes to mind? Aliens? Boyfriend material? A little of both? Well, you're not alone. Take this quiz to find out how much you really know about these crazy creatures—and how to suss out their secrets.

1 Your crush tripped and fell on his face at school. His next thought (after "ouch!") is:
a. "I'm so embarrassed! I can't believe everyone saw me! I want to hide."
b. "At least I didn't knock out a tooth."
c. "What? No blood? That blows!"
d. "No big deal. Everyone makes mistakes."

2 When guys spend the night at a bud's house, they probably spend most of the time:
a. Talking about girls.
b. Sleeping.
c. Daring each other to do stupid stuff.
d. Playing video games and talking all night—about video games, of course.

3 If a boy's really into a girl, he lets her know by:
a. Asking her friends to ask her how she feels about him.
b. Showing up at her house with a red rose.
c. Pretending she doesn't exist.
d. Becoming suddenly very shy when she's around.

4 You're telling a funny story when you notice your crush is frowning. You:
a. Ask if he's OK.
b. Stop talking. He's obviously bored and wishes you'd finish already!
c. Mentally rewind what you just said. Did it sound really stupid?
d. Are secretly flattered. That must mean he's really listening to you!

33

5 When you ask a cutie "What's up?" and he says, "Nothing," what he's actually saying is:

a. "I never know what to say to girls."
b. "I've got to play it cool."
c. "I'm so not interested in you."
d. "Nothing!" Some guys just don't have much to say.

6 The homeroom hottie overhears you telling a friend that you flunked your driving test three times. He starts making jokes about it. Obviously, he:

a. Didn't hear the whole story.
b. Is trying to cheer you up.
c. Is a total jerk, even if he looks like Joe Jonas.
d. Doesn't know what else to say.

7 Your guy's driving to a concert with his friends when he realizes he's taken a wrong turn. He'll probably:

a. Ask someone else to take over driving duty—he's too freaked out about being lost.
b. Stop and ask for directions.
c. Blame someone else in the car.
d. Absolutely refuse to admit he made a mistake and keep driving.

8 You're really mad at your boyfriend. He reacts by:

a. Talking about you behind your back.
b. Writing you a note apologizing for being such a dork.
c. Flying off the handle and stomping off.
d. Mumbling, "Can we just forget about this?"

tip

Wanna impress a guy? Learn his language! If he skateboards, for example, know the difference between a heel flip and a switch.

scoring

friendly fan

To you, boys are such strange creatures: They think differently and even speak their own language, completely foreign to you and your friends. Relax, girlfriend! Stop trying to overanalyze what they say or do, and just take 'em at face value. Chances are you'll get the hang of guy-think pretty fast.

cryptic crusher

Every guy is a potential Prince Charming to you. That's sweet, but your dreamy ideal may be a bit over the top, don't you think? It's hard for some boys to express their emotions. They're expected to act super cool and in charge, remember? If they're at least trying to communicate, then cut the dudes a break.

boy crazy

You love the bad boys—you know, the megamoody hotties. But sometimes these guys can be sweet, shy, and sensitive, too. If your boyfriend doesn't display any caring qualities, even when it's just the two of you, then don't give him a free pass. Maybe he's just not worth your attention!

guy-speak gal

Congrats, you ace guy-talk! You know boys aren't really aliens, but that they have their own way of expressing their feelings (or totally obsessing over things, like skateboarding). Play it cool, sistah. There's no need to gloat that you "get" how they work—boys like to think they can keep girls guessing!

are you a dating disaster?

Do you feel hopelessly goofy around boys? Like you try to say one thing and something totally different—and embarrassing—comes out? Or do you feel most comfy when you're hanging with your crush? Take this quiz to find out what signals you're sending.

1 Your crush asks to borrow your notes from the one day you didn't take any. You say:

a. "No prob! I'll give 'em to you later." Then you spend the next hour copying someone else's notes.

b. "Uh, no, sorry." You don't want to explain. What if he thinks you're a total flake? That would be too embarrassing.

c. "I actually don't have any notes. But do you want to get together later to study instead?"

2 If there's a boy you like, your strategy is to:

a. Pump his friends for info, so you can "accidentally" find yourself in all the same places as your crush.

b. Smile at him if you happen to bump into each other. You don't want to come on too strong.

c. Talk to him whenever you see him.

3 You're walking by your cutie's house for the millionth time, when he suddenly comes outside. You:

a. Run up and say hi—maybe he'll want to hang out with you.

b. Pretend you don't see him and jog around the corner.

c. Smile, wave, and say, "Oh, hi. I didn't know you lived here."

4 When you find out a hottie likes you, you make a point to:

a. Call him. What do you have to lose?

b. Keep your distance. What if he changes his mind after he gets to know you?

c. Try to get to know him. Maybe he and his buds want to chill with you and your pals.

5 Your guy just announced he can't stand Chris Brown, but you think he rocks! You:

a. Tell your crush he's crazy and then list the top five reasons why you think Chris Brown's awesome.

b. Keep quiet. You don't want him to think you two are incompatible.

c. Admit you're Chris's biggest fan. Then ask him what singers he likes.

6 Your biggest worry about dating your dream dude is that:

a. He won't be all that.

b. You'll embarrass yourself without even realizing it.

c. It'll feel like being with just another bud and not a boyfriend.

7 If your friends were to nickname you for the way you act around guys, they'd call you:

a. The Diva—you loooove being the center of attention.

b. The Shadow—when a guy shows up, the real you disappears.

c. Nothing—you don't "act" around guys.

If you go in for a smooch, make sure you aren't all glossed out. Boys don't want to be left wearing your lip goo after a kiss!

scoring

confident with cuties

You can hang with the hotties, no prob. Coolness and confidence are super easy for you, but make sure you don't come off as too self-assured. Some guys—especially shy ones—might be scared of your take-charge attitude. Just be yourself, not a hyped-up, louder-than-life version, and plenty of guys will come running—and stick around for a while!

guy shy

Your sensitivity is totally awesome. Boys probably feel like they can talk to you about anything. They know you'd never laugh at them or roll your eyes, so why don't you do the same for yourself? Stop being so ultra-anxious that you'll do or say something wrong. Relax! So what if you accidentally sneeze in front of the guy or he catches you singing off-key? If he's really the dude for you, he'll be charmed even more.

poised with boys

Wow, you are the real deal. No way would you ever put up a front or try to be someone you're not just to get a guy to like you. You understand that boys are people, too—not some aliens from another planet—and that's what makes you so comfy around every cutie. But give your crush a little extra attention. You're so friendly with everyone, he might need a hint that he's the special one for you.

perfect pals?

You and your best friend spend every possible minute together and share everything. But are the two of you truly in tune? Take this quiz together, keep track of both your answers, and see if you're in sync.

1 You're on a scavenger hunt and are stuck finding the last item. You:
a. Just continue to follow your instincts.
b. Give up.
c. Call your best friend to help.

2 Which stall do you use in a public bathroom?
a. The one closest to the door.
b. One of the middle stalls.
c. The handicapped stall.

3 If you could paint your bedroom any color, it would be:
a. Red.
b. Black.
c. Pink.
d. Blue.

4 A magic genie grants you one wish. You pick:
a. A special device that lets you hear what animals are thinking.
b. A magic potion that makes you irresistible to guys.
c. Be-a-celebrity-for-a-day pill.
d. A crystal ball that shows the future.

5 You win a free airplane ticket to anywhere in the world. Where would you go?
a. France.
b. Morocco.
c. Jamaica.
d. Japan.

6 Your biggest peeve is:

a. People who talk about themselves too much.
b. Stinky feet.
c. Slowpokes.
d. People who don't keep their promises.

7 When you want a snack, you crave:

a. Salty stuff, like chips or pretzels.
b. Sweet stuff, like chocolate or candy.
c. Healthy stuff, like carrot sticks or apple slices.

scoring

Give yourself one point for each question you and your pal answered the same.

your answers:

1. _____
2. _____
3. _____
4. _____
5. _____
6. _____
7. _____

her answers:

1. _____
2. _____
3. _____
4. _____
5. _____
6. _____
7. _____

total answers the same: _____

Practice your listening skills by looking at people when they're talking.

scoring

true twins

5 to 7 points

The verdict is in: You and your best friend are like peanut butter and jelly—you're meant to be together. You probably finish each other's sentences and hate (or love) the same people at school. It's like a spooky psychic thing 'cause you both know what the other is thinking without having to say a word. Other people are sometimes jealous of how amazingly tight you guys are. It's incredibly fun having a friend who's so much like you, so enjoy it!

soul sistahs, sorta

3 to 4 points

You two are supertight and have lots in common. You do weird stuff, like buy the same shirt while shopping separately—on that rare occasion when you're at the mall without each other. But you also have distinct personalities, and that probably helps you get along better than if you were exactly alike. Maybe one is more introspective and the other is more outgoing. Whatever the sitch, you two balance each other out.

vive la différence

0 to 2 points

OK, so you aren't exactly twins, but you guys challenge each other, and that makes the relationship interesting. You each bring something different and fabulous to the friendship. Ever heard the expression, "opposites attract?" Well, it goes for best friends, too—the qualities you respect in someone else may be different from the ones you have. It's about learning, and you two definitely have that in the bag.

friend or boyfriend?

You and your bud hang out all the time. But could you and he be something more?

1 When he e-mails or IMs you, it's usually about:
a. Homework or some funny joke he knows will crack you up.
b. Dating advice. He's always after one girl or another.
c. Nothing in particular. He just likes to chat.

2 He's said before that:
a. You'd be a high-maintenance girlfriend.
b. You'll probably end up married to each other one day.
c. You can be as annoying as his little sister.

3 If you two are hanging out watching TV, he's most likely to:
a. Complain you took the best chair and should move to the floor.
b. Sit kinda close to you on the couch.
c. Sprawl all over you, his feet in your face.

4 If someone assumes you two are dating, your pal:
a. Gets really angry. "Can't a guy and a girl just be friends?"
b. Looks embarrassed and kind of shrugs.
c. Laughs and asks you what you think.

5 When he sees you all dressed up, he:
a. Smiles and tells you how great you look.
b. Gets really awkward and won't look you in the eye.
c. Jokes he didn't recognize you— you look almost human!

6 A friend dishes that your long-time crush is into you! When you tell your boy bud, he:
a. Slaps you a high five and tells you to go for it.
b. Totally changes the subject.
c. Launches into deets of how your dream date is really a dud.

7 When you hang with his friends, he always:
a. Gets kinda protective. He doesn't like them getting too crazy—or too close to you.
b. Makes a point to treat you like one of the guys.
c. Suggests you call some of your friends so everyone can be together.

8 When you ask him who he likes, he's likely to:
a. Shrug and say, "No one."
b. Jokingly say, "You!"
c. Name a few girls, then ask who he's got the best chance with.

9 True or False: When it comes time to pick lab partners, he's more likely to choose you than the class brainiac.

10 True or False: He's called you for no reason, just to say hi.

scoring

1. a. 2; b. 1; c. 3 2. a. 2;
b. 3; c. 1 3. a. 1; b. 3; c. 2
4. a. 1; b. 2; c. 3 5. a. 3;
b. 2; c. 1 6. a. 1; b. 2; c. 3
7. a. 3; b. 2; c. 1 8. a. 2;
b. 3; c. 1 9. True 3 False 0
10. True 3 False 0

scoring

major boyfriend material

24 to 30 points

Your pal showers you with tons of compliments—or he tries to sabotage your relationships with other guys. There's definitely more here than just a good friendship. How do you feel about him? If it's mutual, then suggest you two do something more like a real date—maybe a picnic in the park—to see if sparks fly. Don't worry about losing him as a friend, 'cause if you're as tight as it seems, you'll be able to work through any probs.

more than just a pal

15 to 23 points

One minute he's teasing you, the next he's raving about how great you are. Your boy bud may be on the fence about his feelings for you. His hot-and-cold actions could be fueled by a fear that romance would ruin the friendship. On the other hand, he might flirt with you 'cause he thinks you won't take it too seriously. If you're into this guy as a boyfriend, drop a few hints about the two of you dating. He'll either have no idea what you're talking about, or he'll be thrilled you made the first move!

friends to the end

8 to 14 points

No doubt about it, you've got a solid friendship with this boy. You two are super comfortable with each other and always manage to have a great time. If you're harboring a serous crush on your pal, it's time to face facts: Sometimes a friendship really is just a friendship. If you're wanting a date, it's probably best to look for a different boy, who sees you as both a girl and a friend.

what's your movie role?

Comedy, romance or action? Does it seem like your life's a movie? Take this tell-all quiz and find out which one you star in.

1 Oh no! Your remote control is stuck on one channel. If you're lucky, it's:
a. Cartoon Network—you like a good giggle.
b. The CW—you love all the hot guys and romance.
c. MTV—you can't get enough of those reality shows!

2 You're in charge of this weekend's plans. You suggest:
a. Playing a round of miniature golf.
b. The local planetarium for a night of stargazing.
c. Rock climbing to get the adrenaline pumping.

3 Who's your fave female artist?
a. Lady Sovereign—her lyrics crack you up!
b. Carrie Underwood—heartfelt music that rocks.
c. Rihanna—you can't help but get groovin'.

4 It's time to feed your sweet tooth. The first thing you reach for is:
a. Candy necklaces and lollipop rings.
b. Strawberries dipped in chocolate.
c. An energy bar.

5 What show would you never miss?
a. *Family Guy*—this funny family cracks you up.
b. *Gossip Girl* for its girly drama.
c. *Lost* 'cause it keeps you on the edge of your seat!

49

6 You and your buds are at the mall. What's your first stop?

a. The arcade for some virtual fun with your friends.

b. The bookstore for the latest reads.

c. The sports store to check out new soccer gear.

7. With which superstar would you most like to be friends?

a. Miley Cyrus—she's got great style and a sense of humor.

b. Vanessa Hudgens—a take-charge gal who leaves guys drooling.

c. Ashlee Simpson—she doesn't let anyone push her around.

8 Your friend confides that she really likes your secret crush. You:

a. Half-jokingly say, "Then I guess we'll just have to share him."

b. Tell her it's too late 'cause you liked him first.

c. Swing into super-flirt mode.

9 If you got to pick your leading man, he'd have to be:

a. Dan Humphrey—the adorable and slightly alternative boyfriend of Serena's.

b. Chuck Bass—that bad boy is irresistible!

c. Nate Archibald—this hot jock is the only one who could keep up with you!

10 You find out your best friend blabbed your deepest secret. You:

a. Are furious. You let her know how mad you are with your biting sarcasm.

b. Cry, then plan to teach her something about friendship.

c. Swear not to talk to her until she apologizes.

11 It's date night and you get to pick the DVD. You choose:

a. *Superbad*. The only way to watch this flick is with someone who laughs as hard as you.

b. *The Notebook*. It sets the mood for romance.

c. *Pirates of the Caribbean*. Your guy had better like action and adventure or he's history.

scoring

comedy chick

You'll do anything for a laugh, and everyone loves that about you. You make every situation fun. But just 'cause others expect you to be a joker 24/7 doesn't mean you can't show your serious side, too. Find a balance that suits you. People will appreciate all of you.

romantic leading lady

You live in the moment and want to be with someone who makes your stomach go flip-flop. You want to be the star of your life—and every plot should revolve around true love. Your attitude inspires others, and that makes you a wonderful friend. Be careful, though—you don't wanna stop living in reality. That can set you up for heartache if things don't play out the way you dreamed. Still, keep reaching for the stars: You might just get there.

action hero

Your life is full of action and you're always in the middle of it! You're constantly on the go and that energy motivates others to get moving, too. You go the extra mile to do things others never dared. Although it's in your nature to hop, skip, and jump your way through life, it's all right to take an evening to chill with buds and get geared up for the next go-round.

are you sabotaging your skin?

Do you suffer from zits, dryness, or the greasies? If you don't care for your face the right way, you could be doing more harm than good. Take this quiz to see whether your habits are helping or hurting your complexion.

1 What aggravates acne the most?
a. Eating French fries.
b. Sipping a latte.
c. Munching on a donut.

2 It's possible to shrink your pores.
a. True.
b. False.

3 When shouldn't you use an exfoliating scrub?
a. If you have dry skin.
b. If you have zits.
c. If you have combination skin.

4 If you just picked a pimple, what's the best way to make the nasty sucker disappear?
a. Apply a benzoyl peroxide product.
b. Gently squeeze it again to get rid of all the gunk.
c. Steam your face to open up the pores.

5 Where is the most sensitive skin on your body?
a. Fingertips.
b. Lips.
c. Eyelids.

6 When should you use a moisturizer?
a. Every day.
b. If your skin is flaky.
c. When you get older.

7 At what age is your skin the most vulnerable to damage from the sun?
a. 12 to 15 years old.
b. 16 to 20 years old.
c. 21 to 26 years old.

8 How often should you change your skincare products?
a. Twice a year.
b. Never—stick with what works.
c. Whenever something new hits the store shelves.

scoring

1 b. Sipping a latte.
Acne loves caffeine 'cause it dehydrates you, leaving your complexion parched. That's when your skin shifts into oil-producing overdrive, which can cause even more zits.

2 b. False.
Let's get one thing straight: Your pores are the size they are and that's it. However, you can make them appear smaller by keeping your face clean with toners and mild scrubs. These can help decrease the amount of gunk clogging your pores and make your skin look more crater-free.

3 b. If you have zits.
While there's something weirdly satisfying about sloughing off the top layers of your skin, if you have pimples, steer clear of grainy scrubs. The abrasive beads can expose a zit and spread its bacteria to other areas of your face. Instead, try a chemical exfoliator, such as a cream with alpha-hydroxy or salicylic acid to get rid of pore-clogging flakes.

4 a. Apply a benzoyl peroxide product.

First of all, an unpicked zit heals much quicker than a picked one 'cause the skin hasn't been broken and won't catch more dirt. Your best bet for zapping a popped pimple is to apply a benzoyl peroxide cream to kill the bacteria. Also, put a dab of this on before bed 'cause your skin works to heal itself while you sleep.

5 c. Eyelids.

Your lids and the skin around your eyes are much thinner than the rest of your bod and, therefore, the most sensitive. Plus, with all that blinking, laughing, and finger rubbing, your lids take a beating. Be kind to your peepers with a little eye cream before you go to bed.

6 a. Every day.

All skin types need moisturizer—even oily skin—'cause it's adding water, not oil. "If you have acne, a thick moisturizer can clog your pores," says Ronald Moy, MD, a dermatologist, "so use a moisturizing lotion."

7 a. 12 to 15 years old.

Scary, but true. "The majority of sun damage to the skin happens during the first 15 years of life," says Harold Lancer, MD, a cosmetic dermatologist. "Even a single sunburn when you're a kid will come back and haunt you in your thirties." That might sound like light-years away, but once you see all those wrinkles, freckles and moles, you'll wish you had slapped on some sunscreen when you were still young.

8 a. Twice a year.

When it comes to skincare, think seasonal. Because skin dries out more in the winter, use a less drying cleanser, like a cream or lotion formula, and a slightly heavier moisturizer if needed. For the hotter months, apply a foaming cleanser and oil-free moisturizer. And, don't forget that sunscreen year-round!

what's your fashion style?

Are you an artsy girl, a full-on fashionista, or pretty in pink when it comes to clothes? Take this quiz to find out what fits you best.

1 Your style of inspiration is:

a. A cool painting you saw in a museum.

b. Fashion mags, of course!

c. Reese Witherspoon in both *Legally Blonde* movies.

d. Thrift stores.

e. Whatever's comfortable!

2 To get your crush's attention, you're most likely to choose clothes that:

a. Mix but don't match, so he knows you've got a mind of your own.

b. Look like you stepped off a fashion runway—*très chic*!

c. Are soft and really feminine. You want him to be able to approach you.

d. Get noticed. If everyone's looking at you, he will be, too!

e. Are sporty, so you can keep up with him and his pals!

3 You just earned big bucks for a long night of babysitting. The first thing you do is:

a. Give your room a much-needed makeover.

b. Go on a massive shopping spree.

c. Buy presents for your family and friends.

d. Throw the slumber party to end all slumber parties.

e. Grab your best bud and go miniature golfing.

4 If there was only one TV show you could watch, you'd choose:

a. *Kyle XY.*

b. *Gossip Girl.*

c. *Hannah Montana.*

d. *Heroes.*

e. *Dancing with the Stars.*

5 Your pals tease you because:

a. They never know what funky look you'll pull off next.

b. You can spend your entire allowance at the mall.

c. You're always more dressed-up than they are.

d. You're constantly changing your clothes.

e. You've always hated wearing dresses.

6 For your best bud's birthday, you:

a. Make her a reconstructed T-shirt.

b. Buy her an expensive makeup bag.

c. Bake her a batch of your famous cookies.

d. Edit together a video of your funniest moments caught on tape.

e. Buy her a new video game.

7 The time of year you love the most is:

a. Any holiday. It's an excuse to make some cool decorations.

b. Fall: Back-to-school shopping is the best!

c. Spring: You're all for sunny days and beautiful blooming flowers.

d. Winter: It means jacket, scarf, and hat season.

e. Summer: The more you can do outside, the better.

8 When it comes to shoes, your motto is:

a. "Think fun and funky."

b. "If it costs me, it's got to be worth it."

c. "Everything's better in pink."

d. "Shoes make or break an outfit."

e. "If I can't run in 'em, I won't wear 'em."

scoring

artsy girl

You love putting outfits together. Nothing feels quite right unless it has your unique touch! **Your perfect fit:** Go for eye-catching prints, vintage accessories, and funky skirts with unexpected hems. Try wearing a chic hat and some bold jewelry.

fashionista girl

You share the same fashion sense (and expensive taste!) as your favorite celebs. Your pals trust you to be up on the very latest trends. **Your perfect fit:** Skirts in fluid fabrics and shirts with super feminine necklines look great on you. Add a pair of killer high heels as your signature accessory, and you'll look like you have your own stylist!

girly girl

You love to dress in feminine clothes that match your personality. No jeans and baseball hats for you! You'd wear skirts every day if you could.
Your perfect fit: Flirty miniskirts, delicate tops, and romantic hats to frame your face. Little details like ruffles, ribbons, and flowery prints look great on you—just wear them in moderation!

edgy girl

It's true, you do just want to have fun! You would never be caught in drab colors or with shoes that don't match your outfit.
Your perfect fit: Button-down shirts, cropped pants, and tees in funky prints. Thrift stores are a great place for you to shop because you can always score something unique.

active girl

You crave adventure, and your free spirit attitude is reflected in the clothes you choose. You're sporty, not sloppy!
Your perfect fit: It's all about layering such as pairing a jean jacket with a cool tee underneath. Hip accessories—a wide belt, a chunky bracelet—will never go out of style with you.

do cliques rule your life?

Sure, everyone feels the need to fit in, but are you obsessed with being part of the "in" crowd? See if you're a clique chick.

1 It's time for swim practice again. You hate it, but you forced yourself to sign up because:
a. You love competing, it's the socializing you can't stand.
b. It seems like a good way to meet people.
c. Everyone who's anyone is on the swim team.

2 You seriously need to find a dress for the upcoming school dance. You:
a. Ask your bud if you could borrow something. Why blow your allowance on a dress you'll only wear once?
b. Have your closest pals meet you at the mall...stat!
c. Ask your friends what they think you should wear. You trust their sense of style way more than your own.

3 You won the student council raffle prize of an awesome new mountain bike. You start hearing a rumor that the most popular girl in school is bummed she didn't win. What do you do?
a. Gloat a little—maybe her life isn't so perfect after all!
b. Ask if she wants to give the bike a spin.
c. Give her the bike. Sure it's a little drastic, but this could be just the thing you need to upgrade your social status!

4 The coolest crowd has decided you deserve to sit with them at lunch, but not your best bud, who's waiting at your usual table. You:
a. Turn them down—and tell them just how shallow you really think they are.
b. Say, "Sorry. Maybe some other time."
c. Immediately have a seat—your bud will understand.

5 Your lab partner is the geekiest guy in school, but he's actually pretty nice. When the popular kids start picking on him, you:

a. Ignore them. What do they know?

b. Explain that he's an OK guy, you like him and they should give him a chance.

c. Join in. If they know you and he are friends, your reputation's ruined!

6 When it comes to clothes, you're known for:

a. Totally doing your own thing. Who cares if you look different and people stare?

b. Fitting in. You're not a trendsetter, but you always look your best.

c. Dressing like your pals. Every a.m., you coordinate outfits over the phone.

7 The star of the baseball team asked you out. He's super popular, but not exactly your type. You:

a. Turn him down. Why waste your time if you're not totally into him?

b. Give him a chance. You're open to anything.

c. Immediately get on the phone and tell everyone you're a couple.

8 A group of cheerleaders sees you trying to deal with your bratty little bro at the mall. "You're not related, are you?" one of them sniffs. You:

a. Get defensive. No one's allowed to criticize your bro except for you!

b. Smile and joke, "You should see him on a really bad day."

c. Lie and say, "No way! I'm just babysitting!"

9 For your birthday party, you really want to stay home and have an all-girl slumber party. Two of your friends say they won't come if your party's "lame." You:

a. Immediately uninvite them.

b. Assure them it'll be great. They can even help pick out the movies and munchies!

c. Back off and let them take over the planning.

10 Your teacher caught you passing a note to your pal and read it aloud. You're:

a. Not bothered. You pride yourself on not caring what others think.

b. Mortified. What an invasion of privacy!

c. In serious trouble. You wrote a few things about a friend that you haven't said to her face.

scoring

singular sistah

Your independence is impressive, but before you pat yourself on the back too much, make sure your "Lone Wolf" routine isn't based on a fear of getting involved. Instead of jumping to conclusions that certain people aren't friend-worthy, give them a chance. Join a club or talk to a different group of kids at lunch for a change. Your open-minded attitude might just surprise them—and you, too!

crowd-pleaser

Your supersensitivity makes you a true-blue friend. You'll never turn your back on a pal and you always choose friendships over the clique-of-the-month. Standing up for what you believe in reveals some serious self-confidence, so it's no wonder others are psyched to call you their friend. Continue to take the occasional chance with new people and, in no time, you'll find your group of pals growing.

clique crazed

No one can call you a social slacker. You put tons of energy into your friendships! Although it's cool that your pals mean a lot to you, you've gotta make sure they're not taking over your life. If you're giving up things you love—or pretending to be someone you're not—it might be time to take a step back. Trust your judgment instead of depending on outside approval and you'll see who your buds really are.

how well do you know your best bud?

You and your best friend are super tight—you know all her secrets and she knows yours. Or does she? Put your friendship to the test with this quiz for two.

What to Do
Grab your best friend, some pens, and this quiz. Sit across from each other and answer the questions at the same time—no discussing the answers allowed! Afterward, grade each other's answers.

1 If your best friend won free tickets to any concert, which one would she choose?
a. Kanye West.
b. The Jonas Brothers.
c. Miley Cyrus.
d. Justin Timberlake.

2 a. What's the name of the first guy she kissed?

_____

_____

b. Who's her current crush?

_____

_____

3 What's her middle name? (You have to spell it correctly!)

_____

_____

4 What was her most embarrassing moment ever?

_____

_____

_____

_____

5 Your pal's fave chips are:

a. Salt and vinegar.
b. Sour cream and onion.
c. BBQ.
d. Plain.

6 What's her favorite ice cream?

Vanilla I
Ice Boib)

7 What gift would she love to get from you for her birthday?

a. A big surprise party with all of her buds.
b. The makeup she was eyeing at the mall.
c. A handmade picture frame with a cute photo of the two of you in it.
d. A gift certificate to her fave store—she likes to pick out her own stuff.

8 What size shoe does she wear?

Size 8 women

9 If she won $1,000, what would be the first thing she'd buy?

a picture
maybe

10 In 10 years, your best bud wants to be:

a. Famous.
b. Married.
c. Rich.
d. A mom.

scoring

You earn 2 points for each correct answer, 1 point if it's almost right, and 0 if you were way off. Add up your points and compare your scores. Now see how your friendship rates.

	0 to 7 points	**8 to 14 points**	**15 to 20 points**
you ▼ **0 to 7 points**	Did you two just meet yesterday? Seriously, you're not on the same wavelength at all. Try a little talking—it works!	She's the one in the know. Do you want to be best friends? It's time to start hanging out more and get to know her better.	Uh-oh, either your bud is a stalker or you're awful at friendship. Time for you to make more of an effort if you want to keep this pal.
8 to 14 points	You know your friend better than she knows you. Are you super secretive? Find out what's going on, so you can become better buds.	You are starting to know each other really well. Keep talking! Then try this quiz again in a month—betcha get a way better score.	This is a friend you don't want to lose—she knows everything about you and really cares. Show her how much you appreciate her!
15 to 20 points	You know everything about this girl and she knows nothing about you. It's time to open up and make this a two-sided friendship!	You're an awesome friend and she's pretty good, too. With some more time you guys can bring this friendship to the next level.	Amazing! Either you're both psychic or you are the best of buds. Stick together and keep sharing everything—friends for life!

are you what you eat?

Get the dish on what your food 'tude reveals about you. Take a bite outta this quiz and see how your munching style gives the 411 on your personality.

1 Your breakfast choice is:
a. A sugary donut.
b. A natural granola with fruit.
c. A bowl of cereal with nonfat milk.

2 If you had to pick one spice to add to your pizza sauce, what would it be?
a. Garlic powder.
b. Crushed red pepper flakes.
c. Oregano.

3 When babysitting, you're psyched to see what munchies in the cabinet?
a. Peanuts.
b. Beef jerky.
c. Tortilla chips.

4 You fill your ice cream cone with scoops of:
a. Chocolate chip.
b. Vanilla.
c. Strawberry.

5 When Easter season rolls around, you're happy to find out your chocolate bunny is:
a. Hollow.
b. Solid chocolate.
c. Filled with peanut butter.

6 Your favorite run for the border is:
a. Nachos Supreme with hot salsa.
b. Taco salad.
c. Cheese quesadilla.

7 Your parents are throwing a huge party. Your fave snack sneak is:
a. Black olives.
b. Mixed nuts.
c. Those little pickles.

8 Your soda style is:
a. To drink straight from the can or bottle.
b. To sip from a glass with ice.
c. To pour it into a glass with no ice.

9 Oreos have to be eaten:
a. In one bite.
b. After being dunked in milk.
c. By pulling 'em apart and licking off the cream first.

scoring

1. a. 5; b. 3; c. 1 2. a. 5; b. 3;
c. 1 3. a. 1; b. 5; c. 3 4. a. 3;
b. 5; c. 1 5. a. 1; b. 3; c. 5
6. a. 5; b. 3; c. 1 7. a. 3; b. 1;
c. 5 8. a. 1; b. 3; c. 5 9. a. 5;
b. 1; c. 3

scoring

34 to 45 points

nutty, like party mix

Chaos surrounds your life 24/7. You're really outgoing and social, and you have tons of friends. It's rare for insults to get you down (probably 'cause you're too busy to dwell on them!). The foods you favor reveal that you don't like to pick fights or point out friend's flaws. "You have a tendency to lean on other people to direct you and make decisions for you," says Alan Hirsch, MD, author of *What Flavor Is Your Personality?* (Sourcebooks Trade). "You can overcome that with practice."

21 to 33 points

strong, like a jawbreaker

You should wear a sign that says, "Hello, my name is Ms. Perfectionist." You find it hard to delegate little tasks 'cause you're afraid other people will mess 'em up. Your food choices say you crave order and like to be the best at everything you do.. The downside? "Your family and friends may tell you to lighten up because you even take your hobbies very seriously," says Dr. Hirsch. "You consider yourself very thrifty, but a person who is not fond of you might call you stingy."

9 to 20 points

soft, like a marshmallow

Does your back hurt? Carrying around everyone else's probs has got to take its toll on you. Your food selections show that you are thoughtful, punctual, and cautious—definitely a girl who likes to look before you leap. "You want things to go well, so you tend to worry that they won't," says Dr. Hirsch. "Your friends would not call you care-free, but you see yourself as concerned."

are you waiting for mr. perfect?

Nobody's saying that you have to settle for a bargain-bin boy in the Store of Love. But waiting around for someone who's flawless? That's just as wrong. This quiz will reveal if you're setting your boyfriend-meter way too high—or desperately low.

1 A guy takes you to the movies, but when it's time to buy the tickets, it turns out he doesn't have enough cash. You:

a. Pay for both of you, and tell him he can buy next time.

b. Pay your own way in, but he can forget about a second date.

c. Buy your own ticket—it's not a big deal to you.

2 Your friend wants to set you up on a blind date with her cousin. You tell her:

a. No way. You've seen the photo of him when he was 10 and had braces and glasses.

b. Sure. Your friend wouldn't set you up with her cousin if he wasn't cool.

c. Of course! You'd never turn down a blind date. Who knows? He could be "the one."

3 After a couple of dates, your new guy tells you he doesn't want a serious girlfriend, but he's cool with keeping things casual—a date now and then kind of thing. This means:

a. You'll wait to see how things go. It's too soon to tell if you want to be serious about him anyway.

b. You'll consider bailing on the whole situation. He obviously doesn't appreciate you.

c. You're bummed, but you're not about to complain. You don't want him to think you're needy.

4 You've just had the most horrid haircut and aren't going to the school dance that way. You tell your guy:

a. He should go solo. It's not his fault you can't attend the dance wearing a baseball cap.

b. To ask another girl to the dance. He deserves to have a date, even if it's not you.

c. He'd better not even think of going without you.

5 On your first date, he wants to take you out for a romantic meal, but forgets you're a vegetarian. He feels awful when he takes you to a steakhouse, so you suggest:

a. You can just have the yummy mashed potatoes and side salad—no prob!

b. He can make up for it on your next date by taking you to that incredibly expensive new French restaurant.

c. Going somewhere for a veggie burrito instead.

6 Your boyfriend is stressing about the test you both have in history class. To help him out, you:

a. Offer to study with him the night before. Your notes are much better than his.

b. Let him look on your paper during the test.

c. Wonder why he can't get his act together.

scoring

1. a. 1; b. 3; c. 2   2. a. 3;
b. 2; c. 1   3. a. 2; b. 3; c. 1
4. a. 2; b. 1; c. 3   5. a. 1;
b. 3; c. 2   6. a. 2; b. 1; c. 3

your motto is...

"he's alive, therefore he's dateable."

6 to 9 points

So what if he's not the most thoughtful—he's a boy, and boy equals fun, right? Time to change your boyfriend attitude, 'cause you deserve more. No one has to put up with a guy who's constantly late, forgets to call, and can't dress himself. Since it's not always easy to choose being solo over being with a cute dude who isn't ideal, try this exercise in self-worth: Make a list of your good points, like how you're smart, how you make people laugh, how you can do magic tricks, whatever. Look over the list and remember, those are the things about you that your friends adore. The right guy for you will also love these things. You can have it all. Promise.

10 to 14 points

"he's not perfect, but I'll try him."

You understand that a guy can't be perfect all the time, but you also demand a certain level of respect. If he's got stinky sneakers or he's a fashion disaster, you can deal. You just need him to be a good guy. But if he's treating you badly or forgets how to spell your name, he's yesterday. It's the same list of requirements you'd apply to your best friend. And just as you'd never diss your friend for a beauty blunder, you can forgive your guy his faults and move on. You've learned that the secret to a great relationship is to base it on fairness. With your dating skills, you could be well on your way to romantic bliss!

15 to 18 points

"if he's got a flaw, he's outta here."

Zac Efron is taken. So are Chris Brown and Chace Crawford. And even if you did get five minutes with a "dream guy," you'd probably find plenty wrong with him, too. Why are you so picky? Deep down, could it be that you're afraid of getting close to a guy? Maybe you're setting your sights so high because you know there's not a dude alive who can match your standards. Not every boy out there is set to break your heart, so give an Everyday Joe a chance. Next time you're attracted to the boy next door, don't tell yourself it could never be. Give your heart a chance to get to know him. You might find that some of his flaws are the most adorable things in the world.

gossip much?

**Are you more plugged in than a toaster?
The urge to dish can be deliciously tempting,
especially when you know people's secrets. But
do you spill too much?**

1 You grab a computer and realize the cutie who just left forgot to log out of his e-mail. His inbox is staring at you. You:

a. Cruise through the messages and read everything but the junk mail.

b. Click the "sign out" button, then go polish your halo.

c. Peek at a few e-mails.

2 A group of your friends are chatting quietly in the hall. When you approach, they:

a. Start talking about something else.

b. Say hi and keep talking freely.

3 After being MIA all spring break, your nemesis shows up 10 pounds slimmer. You hear rumors about a fat camp. What do you do?

a. Announce it to everyone even though you have no idea whether it's true or not.

b. Bring it up while texting your best friends.

c. Keep your mouth shut. You despise her, but also kinda feel bad for her.

4 A super smart girl in your math class is whispering to a friend. You think you hear her admit to cheating, but you're not 100% sure. You:

a. Tell yourself you must have heard wrong—she wouldn't do that.

b. Spread the word—that's how she's setting the curve!

c. Want to tell someone, but you aren't completely sure what she said, so you zip your lips.

5 A friend e-mailed you a hot piece of gossip and asks you not to tell anyone. You:

a. Delete it immediately!

b. Keep it in your mailbox, but don't say a word…yet.

c. Quickly forward it to your best buds. You can't just sit on a story this good!

6 You spot the guy who dumped and devastated your BFF locking lips with a new girl. You:
a. Whip out your camera phone, snap a pic, and show everyone.
b. Catch up with your pal tomorrow to tell her what you saw.
c. Ignore it. She doesn't need to hear about it.

7 You're at a really rich friend's house and you accidentally see her parents' bank statement. You tell:
a. Nobody—you feel bad for snooping.
b. Just one friend—otherwise you'd burst.
c. A few friends—immediately!

8 The rumor is that the new girl was kicked out of her last school for stealing. You:
a. Try to get to know her.
b. Tell all the girls why they shouldn't leave their purses unattended.
c. Quietly ask people what they know about her.

9 You overhear a popular girl fighting with someone on her cell. How much of the conversation do you listen to?
a. The entire thing, 'cause you dawdle by your locker, trying to hear every last detail.
b. As little as possible. You don't really care about her personal life.
c. As much as you can until you've gotta get to your next class.

10 In a game of Truth or Dare, your friend admits to a crush on the dorkiest guy in school. She swears you to secrecy. Will you blab?
a. You'd never do that to her.
b. You'd have to tell just one other friend.

scoring

1. a. 3; b. 1; c. 2 2. a. 3; b. 1
3. a. 3; b. 2; c. 1 4. a. 1; b. 3;
c. 2 5. a. 1; b. 2; c. 3 6. a. 3;
b. 2; c. 1 7. a. 1; b. 2; c. 3
8. a. 1; b. 3; c. 2 9. a. 3; b. 1;
c. 2 10. a. 1; b. 3

scoring

gossip guru

You've got the goods, from the entire make-out history of all your buds to what size bra your mom wears. "Dirt" is your middle name. Thanks to gossip-friendly tech, rumors are hard to avoid. But spreading untrue or hurtful info—even if it's spicy or about someone you detest—goes against good gossiping etiquette. Remember, gossip gals usually don't hang on to friends for long 'cause they end up hurting too many people.

only human

Listening to juicy stories about other people is like watching *The Real World*—you just can't help getting sucked in, even though you know it's not good. There is always the temptation to blurt out your secrets to make everybody in the room go, "Whoa! No way!" But you're usually able to hold your tongue. Sometimes, though, you just have to tell one or two close friends, whom you swear to secrecy, of course!

secret sistah

You spill all your secrets to just one source—like your diary. Even hot tidbits that you sometimes like hearing won't cross your lips. That kind of respect for secrecy is admirable. Your friends know their private convos are for your ears only, which means they're more willing to open up and ask for your opinion on really personal stuff. Your friends are lucky to have you. Now, go hide that diary somewhere super safe.

are you jealous?

Is your envy holding you back? Or have you learned to tame the green-eyed monster?

1 Your best friend shows up for the dance looking fabulous in a new outfit! You:
a. Suddenly feel insecure about your look, but quickly shrug it off and compliment her.
b. Feel your stomach drop. Can't you ever be the pretty one?
c. Are happy that you and your pal both look so amazing tonight.

2 Your guy casually mentions that he thinks Amanda Bynes is really talented. You say:
a. "Sure, for a comedic actress," even though you like her, too.
b. "Do you think she's better looking than me?"
c. "I know. She's great."

3 Your two best buds are chatting about a shopping trip they took over the weekend without you. You say:
a. "Um, hello! I wasn't doing anything. Next time call me, OK?"
b. "I can't believe you guys! I thought we were friends, but I guess not."
c. "So did you get anything cool? How soon can I borrow something?"

4 A cute guy asks you out and you say yes. Before your date, you find out he asked out someone else first, but she said no. You:
a. Reluctantly go anyway. Maybe he's not crushing on you, but you could still have a fun time.
b. Cancel the date. It's too embarrassing to be the second choice.
c. Go out and have a blast. End of story.

5 Your secret crush is dating someone else. One day his girlfriend randomly says she loves your earrings and asks where you got them. You tell her:

a. The mall, but you don't name the store.

b. You bought them in Europe so she won't even look for 'em.

c. Exactly where they are in the store and then ask where she got her shoes.

6 You were totally convinced you scored the lead in the school musical, but a freshman got the part. When everyone goes to congratulate her, you:

a. Go home and cry on your pillow before e-mailing her a congrats note.

b. Tell her it's a perfect part for a beginner because it's such a lame production.

c. Put aside your disappointment and say you know she'll do a great job.

tip

If you often find yourself envious, try this: Write down 10 things that make you feel good about yourself. Now, pat yourself on the back! And think about it, maybe someone is jealous of you!

scoring

everyday envy

Sure you get jealous sometimes, but who doesn't? But you never let your envy of others get out of hand. You might wish you were the star of the play or the object of your crush's affections, but when you're not, you don't get all snarky. Hey, you might even let it inspire you to try harder! Learning to turn negative emotions into something positive is a really mature way of handling tough situations. We all get jealous sometimes, but it's how we handle it that matters. Keep up the good work!

green-eyed girl

Uh-oh, jealousy is getting the best of you way too often. Of course, it's hard watching other people get the kudos and compliments you want, but remember, it's all about being the best you can be. Spending too much time eyeing what other people have can blind you to the things you already have. The next time you feel the green-eyed monster creeping up, take a deep breath and remind yourself of all your strengths and blessings. It'll take some practice, but eventually you'll get out of the habit of constantly complaining!

just not jealous

Your lack of envy is another example of your awesome personality! Laid-back and truly not competitive, you have an easy time remembering that other people's accomplishments don't take away from your own successes. So what if your best friend looks super hot or if someone else aces every test? You realize you can't spend your life comparing yourself with others, and you can't be the best at everything—you're good at being you. Congrats!

what are your secret skills?

The way you deal with your day says a lot about your natural talents—and how you can use your mind to get anything you want! Take this quiz to find out which side of your brain you're using.

1 It's time for school and you're still searching your closet for something to wear. You pick:

a. Jeans, a tee, and your sneaks. You're all about comfort!

b. A vintage dress with tons of cool accessories.

c. The same mini you wore a few days ago, but dressed up with a bright scarf as a belt.

2 You're running late for school, so you:

a. Beg a friend to pick you up on her way. That'll give you a few minutes for your final beauty touches.

b. Dash to the bus stop, hoping you don't miss it. Why didn't your stupid alarm go off this morning?

c. Ask your mom to drive you—you're usually not late.

3 The dance committee is calling for volunteers and you're so there! You sign up to:

a. Do the decorations. You picture the gym decked out in a crazy underwater theme!

b. Do whatever. You just want to be involved.

c. Organize all the other volunteers. Why didn't anyone else think of that?

4 It's lab day in science class and you're getting graded on your experiment. You:

a. Grab your book and read all about it before you even put your goggles on.

b. Read a little bit about the reaction, then ask your partner to help you get it right.

c. Get to work—you're pretty sure you can wing it.

5 You've had a really long day, but you still have tons of homework. You:

a. Try to do it, but you keep thinking about your crush. Sometimes it's hard to focus on schoolwork when your mind is somewhere else.

b. Focus and get most of it done before *Gossip Girl* starts. You can't miss a week of your fave show.

c. Study until you're finished. There's something really satisfying about completing an assignment.

6 Your mom asked you to pick up some stuff she needs for dinner. You:

a. Get everything on the list—you even found some stuff on sale, awesome!

b. Pick up all the things your mom wants and a bag of chips for yourself. You totally deserve it!

c. Decide you want tacos for dinner instead. You buy all the fixings—your mom won't mind!

7 After school your buds can usually find you:

a. Playing sports or at a club meeting. You like being part of a group.

b. At play rehearsal or in the art room. You just have to be creative.

c. Working on the newspaper or yearbook. Or making sure your homework gets done early—yeah!

8 Your parents left a note explaining they won't be home until late, so you're on your own for dinner. You make:

a. Frozen pizza. Nothing could be better!

b. A new recipe you found in a cookbook—you love to try new stuff.

c. Mac 'n cheese.

scoring

1. a. 1 b. 2; c. 3 2. a. 2 b. 1; c. 3 3. a. 2 b. 3; c. 1 4. a. 1 b. 3; c. 2 5. a. 2 b. 3; c. 1 6. a. 1 b. 3; c. 2 7. a. 3 b. 2; c. 1 8. a. 1 b. 2; c. 3

scoring

two-sided babe

19 to 24 points

At school, you like art, but you're not bad at science either! In love, it's hard to decide between that super-smart sweetie and the quiet, artistic hottie. With friends, they love the way that you're always up for dancing or a study group. Style-wise, you like clothes that are trendy and popular, but you own 'em by adding a funky belt, scarf, or jewelry that's totally you! For a future career, pursue architecture or medicine.

right-minded miss

13 to 18 points

At school, you totally love art and dance is definitely your thing, but math and science are a little hard for you. Sometime it's a struggle to get assignments done on time (maybe 'cause you're too busy writing poetry!). In love, you need a guy who's as creative and fun as you are! With friends, they rely on you for cool ideas, like dressing up 80s style and singing karaoke. Style-wise, your closet is a mix of great old stuff and funky faves. It's no big deal for you to change your nail polish—or hair color—to match what you're wearing. For a future career, consider acting, singing, or teaching the arts.

left-brain lady

8 to 12 points

At school, you're into logic and things that compute, like math and science. But that doesn't mean you do badly in English or art! In love, you want a like-minded left-brain boy, so look for a super-smart and way-cute boy to be your guy. With friends, they know you're the person to go to with any kind of prob—school, boys, or family. Style-wise, you're more practical but you will dress up for the right occasion. For a future career, consider medicine or law.

is your friendship at the end of its road?

Take this quiz to see if your friendship is a one-way ride to nowhere.

1 At lunch, your pals crack up about the time you accidentally snorted milk through your nose...two years ago. You:

a. Laugh as hard as they do. It was pretty funny.

b. Roll your eyes. How many times do you have to hear that story?

c. Beg them to keep their voices down, then start teasing them about all the geeky things they've done.

2 You and your best buds have had a Friday night sleepover as long as you can remember, but a cool girl from homeroom just invited you to a party. You:

a. Bail on your pals. You guys only hang out because there's nothing else to do.

b. Ask if you can bring your friends along.

c. Tell her you'll have to pass. You don't want to hurt your friends' feelings.

3 You're hanging with your friends in the library when your crush walks in. You:

a. Pretend you dropped your pencil and duck under the table until he passes.

b. Wave him over.

c. Spend the rest of the period passing notes to your girls about how hot he looks.

4 You scored the winning goal for your soccer team! When your crowd runs onto the field to congratulate you, you:

a. Introduce them to all your teammates.

b. Explain you're going to celebrate with the rest of your team, but you'll catch up with them later.

c. Feel annoyed. Can't they just give you some space?

89

5 One of your pals just got the exact same haircut as you. You:

a. Tell her you love it. You've always thought she had awesome style.

b. Send her a snarky IM, telling her to get a life!

c. Barely even notice. You guys constantly copy each other.

6 Your mom invited your BFFs to dinner without your knowing. You're:

a. Psyched. You have tons to catch up on.

b. Irked. Your mom should have asked you first.

c. Hoping she'll also let them stay the night.

7 When you and your friends walk home from school, you usually talk about:

a. Weird or annoying stuff that happened that day.

b. All the crazy, fun things you did last school year.

c. The cool people you wish you were friends with.

scoring

1. a. 2; b. 1; c. 3 2. a. 1;
b. 3; c. 2 3. a. 1; b. 3; c. 2
4. a. 2; b. 3; c. 1 5. a. 3;
b. 1; c. 2 6. a. 3; b. 1; c. 2
7. a. 3; b. 2; c. 1

scoring

still fitting in with your friends

17 to 21 points

Congrats! Your connection with your buds is sized just right! You've struck a balance of staying tight with each other while making new friends and trying out different activities. Because none of you is freaked about the relationship changing, chances are, you won't outgrow each other.

clinging to your crowd

12 to 16 points

It's great you and your BFFs are super comfy around each other, but could you also be using each other as an excuse to avoid making new friends? It may seem scary, but remember, your new friendships don't have to replace your old ones. You can never have too many friends.

too big for your BFFs

7 to 11 points

All good things come to an end, even great friendships. Sure, it's sad when you feel like you've hit a wall with your buds, but just think how exciting it'll be to meet some new friends. And, hey, who says you can't still value all the great times you've shared with your past pals?

index

photo credits: